Random Thoughts

Random Thoughts

Seven Days in December

Glen Harris

Strategic Book Publishing and Rights Co.

Strategic Book Publishing and Rights Co., LLC
USA | Singapore
www.sbpra.net

ISBN: 978-1-68235-570-1

Disclaimer

I do not like the idea of writing this disclaimer but, I feel in a world where coffee cups are marked with warnings about their contents' temperatures this must be stated. This book is my thoughts on paper. If you like this book I am elated and thank you for your patronage, if you do not like this book I am not sorry I wrote it, and I advise you to carry on and avoid trying to ruin my life or the lives of the ones I love and care for. In no way are my publishers, affiliates, myself, or any combination of these parties responsible for anyone's actions while reading or after reading this book. Read and consume knowledge at your own risk and have a nice day!

Glen Harris

Preface

This book has gone through many revisions and edits over the years. I originally called my first draft '100 pages' as a title, but I did not like the format. Finally I settled on 'endeavors to comprehend', but after self-publishing it some readers wanted some type of chapter format. After some time and taken my readers into consideration I took the advice of one of my marketers to break it up into days. The new name of the book is 'Random thoughts, Seven days in December', I know it is a bit verbose; however, the name expresses the book well.

Monday

Each person's reality, determined by experiences and personality, necessitates the interpretation of truth, morals, and wickedness. When any person is exposed to the conditions of life, lessons are learned, passions are ignited, aversions are formed. A plethora of factors, coupled with individual ideology and experience, leads people to find qualities they have in common with others. The groups we interact with create their own worlds and in turn their own realities that may seem rooted in universal truths but in fact are constructs of like-minded individuals agreeing on commonly accepted concepts creating the illusion of correctness. Thus, our realities are our interpretation of situations, perceived as legitimate beliefs, and are influenced by what we feel and think we know. Our realities are not broad, practical ideas, inclusive in nature. They serve our inflexible pride, making truth obscure, compromising morals, and letting wickedness go unchecked. One side in a conflict will, unfortunately, implement action, born of stubborn will, push a false perfection, and insist it be obeyed despite its consequences on others. This dogmatic opposition will lead to conflict, unhindered by basic ethics once intense emotions start to drive resolve.

*

An intelligent person admires others
and learns what
they can from them or recruits
fundamental
individuals to complete the task at hand.
A good person does whatever is needed
to make ends
meet to the best of their abilities.
A foolish person looks on everyone with
envy for what
they lack the skill to do, or the courage
to do, or what
they will not do.

*

Your enemies weaknesses
are your strengths; if you
exploit them properly, your enemies'
strengths will mean little.

*

This world has created people who have no self-esteem or self-worth. They idolize the latest fads and exhaust every resource to alterations toward that end. When the others, who cannot afford such luxuries, look upon them, they feel great envy and tend to brood over what they do not have. They fill their minds with empty hopes, never appreciating themselves for who they are, always wishing they were someone else.

*

There are moments...
When life's passing seem to be
summed up easily:
tedious repetition.
Days, weeks, months, years,
Changes are subtle...
For some this is blissful.
For some this is unbearable.
Some use these times for reflection, meditation,
creativity, growth of the spirit.
Some take this time as a reason for change,
any change,
to help counter the boredom.
Time and life have a way of informing
you that although
life can seem as if change is subtle, it is,
in truth, change
all the same. In time, a few subtle
changes can become a
large change for good or bad.
Be leery of moments of enticing pleasures, sweet
temptations of the flesh, drugs,
greed, or violence that
often make diversions, that for
a time, give meaning

through entertainment. One can
lose one's spirit,
enthralled in these activities, and can be
lost in their life
until its end.
Trying times can be naturally brought
about or by one's
own actions.
Choose wisely!
It is no guarantee that a prudent choice
will lead to a
good outcome, but it is always better to have an
idea that
fails than to leave your life to
turbulent chance when
choices spurred by the moment,
fueled by instinct, can
lead to unknown dark places more
often than a wise
choice. Without wisdom to help guide
you out of dark
places you will be lost and
at the mercy of what luck
can provide.

*

Poetry is many things to many people. To me, poetry is a group of words that speak to readers, bringing them to a point of awe or a sudden epiphany long overdue. Some poetry does not appeal to me, but I cannot pass judgment and call it folly. In short it is not the poetry or the poet, but the idea conveyed successfully to individuals who can appreciate and understand the significance for what it is and draw some knowledge, pleasure, or debate from it.

*

There are days…
Long and lonely days
When in a crowd I feel sad and alone
When tears unnoticed fall from inside
pains rising
There are days...
When it's easier to follow the lost..
Crowded masses flow like water,
controlled by
forces unchallenged
Crossing dangers in which some
will perish, and all
know
Luck being our only safe harbor
There are days...
When all I need is to be loved
When no one is around, I must turn an
look to only
one
I look in the mirror and smile
Not from vanity, not for selfish aspiration
I tell the person in the mirror, "I love you"
When no one else will

*

Our greatest enemies are not necessarily
the ones
we have wronged in life but also
the ones we have
loved and failed.

*

Understanding someone is like crossing a vast cavern. Bridges must be built in order to traverse hazardous features that only the truly vigilant may navigate. Even with great bridges two individuals may pass each other in the night, oblivious, and reach the other side bewildered. In this situation, it is easy to make a foolish assumption, which is the very foundation of prejudice.

*

A truly intelligent person knows
that they know
nothing.
A truly wise person knows
that there is always more to
learn.
A truly pious person knows
to look for fault in oneself
and not others.

*

The fading hope of one's desires can cut deep,
forcing
one to search outside of safety
for satisfaction.

Creatures of comfort but
powerfully creative; when
faced with a perilous situation,
great minds and small
minds are often measured by the sum of
circumstances, after the fact, rather than
by individual
attempts to categorize.
Little more than the experiences of
our lives, what else
is life but decisions and results? A trek
down a stretch
of road riddled with turns and alternatives
that bring
us to points sometimes good, sometimes bad.
We all live by chance; even our best
laid plans may fail.
Plan for the future, appreciate the moment
and learn
from the past.
Tomorrow holds no promise;
accept uncertainty.

*

We often decipher with past experiences and bring lessons learned into our lives to counter repetitive mistakes that caused us despair. What we neglect to discern most in life is that sometimes our limited experiences cannot be applied to every situation we encounter, and more often than not unfamiliar circumstances brings new dangers undefined by our experience. When our past leaves us lacking the information we need to act, we find ourselves in the dark, dealing with, learning from, and categorizing new contingencies. Survive this and you are awarded with information vital for victory in the future. Fail your challenge and the severity of your loss is equal to resources you levied. Such is the journey of life for us all.

*

With hopelessness lies and end. With hope there always lies a path toward success or safety. Does it not seem that hope, and hopelessness are two sides of the same coin? The two words represent so much in terms of the human spirit, yet they limit our own beliefs to natural philosophies of the world or the luck we so often lack. It would be enlightening if hope and hopelessness were replaced by understanding, tolerance, and kindness. With these words hope, and hopelessness would have no place in this world. One more impoverished person, one more useless war, or one more hopeless situation would not require hope. What better way to tear at a persons' soul than to give them reason to hope when all that is needed is understanding, tolerance, and kindness. The responsibility of each person lies in the hands of those who can support themselves as well as care for others without strain. However, human beings cling to the same nature they scorn. We prove that we are just animals, as they know all too well the despair of lonely survival that leads to the coin of hope and hopelessness.

*

The savagery of war is best described with this definition. When we as a race realize that war itself is cruel, merciless, and in-human, then we will learn the package of war brings horror unparalleled. To civilize a concept whose very meaning calls for carnage is a poor excuse for not exhausting every effort to end any and all confrontations with tolerance, and understanding. This only proves that we are animals, guided by deep-rooted instincts to destroy rather than reason. Not to mention the self- righteousness that we dare claim the right to being a great civilization.

*

Tuesday

A naked human would not last long in the jungle without their precious technological advancements. Like all animals our natural gift gives us an edge. The cheetah has its speed, the elephant has its mass, the ant has its order, and the human has its mind. For better or for worse, no animal has yet to truly escape its nature. We all work within the confines of the abilities given to us by nature to persevere. Simply put, we are no more and no less than nature's intention.

*

It is a sad fact of life that those
who are noticeably
different in society are treated dis-similarly
and must
establish their worth in order to be
accepted.
When you are unlike most people, be prepared
for prejudice.

*

A person wills whatever they can imagine
into existence
with effort, resources, and need.

*

Whenever you have been branded
the villain in any
situation, expect malicious treatment.

*

Unpleasant thoughts give rise to
unpleasantness personified.

*

Casting cold thoughts, forging new despair from my own existence. Dreading each coming day, each moment, and each second. Knowing one deed always leads to another and another. Depression and paranoia have me in their clutches. I cringe in corners, hiding from myself. I wince when others reach out to help me. My choices are simple, submit or fight, but I must choose soon because it will not be long before I am abandoned by those around me or by my own reasoning.

*

In the interest of peace let no one
stand alone when the
tyranny of malicious hordes falls
upon them.
No greater person is there than
one who joins another in

hopeless battle against hungry
forces bent on impossible goals.

*

The suffering of the world is often caused by the limit's others impose. Thinking that although we all are different everyone should conform to the same values is closed mindedness. Though morals may seem universal in nature, in different surroundings and belief systems, life differs. With this truth, each place, each person's morals, and values evolve differently. No set of rules on one subject can govern any large group of people truly fairly.

*

The righteous have the choice to avoid temptation and slipping occasionally into sin. They struggle to keep good hearts for immortality. Their lives are hardened by the strife, which often are monotonous task given to them by the nefarious to empower the tyranny of the same.

The empty person is destitute of belief and void of ambition. They follow the flow of the tide and die for the beliefs of the nefarious and righteous. They are, in essence, reeds bending in the blowing wind.

The nefarious have the spoils of the weak at their feet, the strong righteous person at their side, and the convenience of apathy to help rule with absolution. They indulge in diversions that destroy the soul and cause anguish and despair for the recipient.

Thus, the immoral behavior of the nefarious is their asset used in the monotonous struggle of the righteous, and the control of the destitute.

*

Time is a sobering, unavoidable fact. Knowledge is the path to understanding. Ignorance is an excuse used by the unintelligent. Use your time wisely to eliminate ignorance through knowledge to avoid contingencies that the unintelligent would normally fall prey to.

*

Whenever you reach the pinnacle of a bountiful situation, prepare to defend your status if defendable, change your situation if changeable, and accept your decline from distinction with dignity, for you have no choice but to descend in time once you have reached your zenith in order to give others a chance at glory.

*

We all harbor prejudice thoughts, but their depth manifest itself during times of choice of the company we keep. When you find yourself in the company of people who view foolish behavior as a pious right and turn their frustrations on other groups with degrading prattle and violent mischief, you have joined sides with the horror of blind prejudice personified. Fatuity leads groups of fools to say things and performing acts that only serve to create greater barriers between people and make amends improbable. Prejudice is the very foundation of misunderstanding one another through ignorance and the very heart of bigotry.

*

The emptiness of life forces us all to believe in something to keep from being completely alone.

*

Our greatest people seem to display great weaknesses. The truth is that we all have weaknesses. It is just our greatest expectations of our greatest people that are unrealistic. The strongest and weakest of us all make mistakes to fit their situation and status in life. Put yourself in peril for massive gain and your rewards may be legendary, your failure, costly. Always choose safely and your safe gain will all most always equal your safe loss.

*

Only blind luck will push you to
greatness when you
seek safety and normality.

*

In life, there comes a time when we must face fate. When the terrible makes its presence known and we must confront it or survive. Choices between confrontation and survival have to do with the situation and people, how much we are willing to sacrifice-or whom. Some choices are for the worst now or worst later. Some we hope are good but never work out; others are surprises, for good or bad;

and others still are repulsive decisions that take us to places we wanted to be all along in the end. We struggle always to learn so much from our mistakes and the mistakes of others. We push and toil to make life meaningful and bountiful. We try to escape easy death when caught in its clutches and fight for each breath, prolonging agony in the dark for the sake of hopeless wishes. We jostle in the direction that blind luck leads, programmed to push on rather than emulate the deceased. If one thing is certain, it is that the universe knows nothing and everything of our jaunt, and in the end, all will be revealed or forever unanswered.

*

Sometimes I understand tyrants. Waves of fury feed my soul until ignition! I try to think of pleasant subjects, but my mind won't let go. I brood over situations long past and force others to bend to my will. Dreaming of revenge, I find myself taking pleasure in others' pain to ease my own inadequacies. These times seem long and often cause me to have fits of rage that make me feel weak and hopeless in the dark. Then I slowly start to realize my folly; fury has me. I return to my benign nature and calm myself with common sense. I exult in my clarity, finally seeing my mistake of feeding my fury and wanting to act on such fatuity. Deep-down inside, history has taught me that only monsters feed evil passions to conclusions too often recognized as tyrannical atrocities.

*

In order to advance one must move. When one moves one relocates into new territory. New territory is unknown; this invites danger, blameless or malicious in nature. One could seek safety by never moving, never challenging, and live life safely crossing the threshold of life unscathed. In everyone is the need to grow, learn, succeed, and take risk. We grow by our mistakes and gain knowledge from lessons learned. We move forward and grow when we take risk, we grow stagnant when we are too cautious, when the danger of risk keeps us from reaping rewards of new unknowns and from knowledge that might bring us happiness or success when one of our journeys is complete.

*

The regulation of situations for conscientiousness or safety should never be too complicated. Too many rules governing complicated situations brought on by numerous repetitive attempts by individuals bent on control rather than acceptance make the world an enigma. Sometimes you should accept the consequences of your plight instead of exhausting resources to regulate the situation, in retrospect creating problems requiring control anew. Choose wisely or choose foolishly: The outcome of your plight equals chance when over-complicated by regulations or laws clouded by simple conscientiousness.

*

In war, it is sad to realize that in the end, after
believing we are serving the greater good,
that we are
contributing to the same atrocities
that made the
losing side seem like tyrants.

*

Virtuous, beneficial intent; exceptionally hard
work;
relentless goal-oriented pursuits;
and uncanny, rare
talents arc no guarantee for fame or success
but rather
intricate pieces of the elusive puzzle
of prosperity.

*

If occasionally in the mist of confusion, you come in and solve the problem at hand, you can be rest assured that you are surrounded by people who try. If often you come into a group of confused people and solve their problems, both big and small, it is almost certain that you are surrounded by victims of sloth or true fools.

*

In my time I have felt enough pain and caused enough to know that emotions are not just an asset but weapons, so powerful at times that even the wrong words can cause emotional damage as destructive as a blade to skin. Words pierce the good hearts the easiest because they grow without fear of suffering. Such hearts grow without dread, but we all are constantly exposed to those who wish to see such love of goodness burst into pieces of despair. This, however, would not end the goodness of such a person, except through the long journey along roads of understanding and care; these journeys are often impeded by the limited trust of involved individuals or the hardened pride of the stubborn.

*

I feared facing reality. As a child, I always did something with my time to occupy myself with my imagination. The outside world to me was a step into a cold and barren place. I wondered about reality sometimes when I was looking at the sky or listening to music. Reality frightened me because it was not always a pleasure. Drawing and writing took my fear away, but I knew that I could never truly escape. Even now, reality is bigger, faster, and always unyielding. Even more it can hurt the heart as well as the mind. In this world, a peaceful dreamer can become lost; although reality is a hard thing to face up to, it is up to us to make it resemble our greatest dreams and ambitions.

*

You have an uneasy choice in life when wronged: forgive or punish. Remember always that forgiveness is absolutely absolving one for deeds done, and once given cannot be retracted without consequences.

Punishment is revenge; you can seek it through the justice system or take matters into your own hands for personal retribution, but this also carries with it certain consequences. Whatever you choose, know that nothing comes without its price, and no single answer can be applied to every situation.

*

I woke up this morning
But still I did not wake
I ate breakfast
Kissed my family
But still I did not wake
I worked and solved problems
I laughed, I talked, and was concerned
But still I did not wake
I returned to my home
Relaxed with my family
But still I did not wake
I went to bed, held the love of my life close
I dreamt of tomorrow, of faraway lands
Of lovers pass and lustful temptations
Of dreams come true for those I care about
Fulfillment of my own dreams
I woke up this morning
But still I did not wake

*

The company that you keep, the family and friends you hold dear, are reflections of who you really are.

*

The pursuit of perfection is the endeavor of fools plagued by disappointment in themselves, fueled by criticism from others, to make themselves seem flawless. Do your best and exult in your efforts and the efforts of others. Leave perfection to fools.

*

Too often are people obsessed with reward instead of process. Apply yourself to the task at hand, reach for the next; when a portion is completed, look still for the next stage. Complete your journey and the reward will always be accomplishment. Feel good about what you have finished and know you have succeeded because you can say, "I did that."

*

Wednesday

Hope is best defined in the measurement of
hopelessness stemming from an
endeavor to create a
successful outcome which from failure
has bleak or
terminal consequences.

*

When you transgress against someone, expect someone to transgress against you. If you are at peace with everyone around you, expect to be transgressed against without provocation. Know with absolute certainty that the world is not fair, and you can always depend on some bad times and some good times, but never let cruel loathsome individuals influence you to a path of transgression without provocation. Walk a path of peace to be an example for all to know that despite what you have been through you is not a product of circumstances but rather a free thinker who chooses for themselves what they can achieve.

*

Emotions evoke passions that create both stable and temporary situations that have outcomes reflective of anyone's best guess. Logic is too passionately arid to apply to every situation, but it helps control emotions gone awry. True logic can call on systematic problem solving that, in the end, can be morally unacceptable. Between logic and emotions, resolution can only come from compromise. If no middle ground can be agreed upon than conflict is the logical inevitability. Brought on by emotion; conflict is the logical answer for passionate beings to settle debates. This, however, does not make it the right answer, but rather and emotional equation carried out to its logical conclusion.

*

Heroes and villains are victims of circumstance.
Heroes help write history books
while villains are
defined by them.

*

We often forget to be thankful and
relish what good
we have in our lives.
When we wish for something more when
circumstances are agreeable, it is simply greed.

*

Guided by fear, one may choose to avoid perilous paths to find safety. Learning begins in unknown territory, which always invites danger that, in essence, should be feared. This, however, is no reason to follow the norm and seek known safety. We learn and grow by pushing forward into the void of the unknown. If gain is for achievement of knowledge for everyone who wish to learn, it is worth braving the dangers. If it is for your enjoyment and nothing or little can be gained accept diversion, it is your life and your decision. Remember always that we are all defined by our actions, and they carry us all into history, where we are labeled useful, entertaining, useless, or forgotten; most of us are forgotten.

*

I know it is better to follow a lonely,
dangerous path
that may lead to doom to achieve
my goals than to
walk in crowded masses, leaving all destiny to
chance.

*

The very essence of the unknown can drive the masses to be controlled by strong wills who focus not on death and consequences but on control and power. With power given to them by the compliant minority and the silent malcontent of the weak majority, a body of people can be controlled for generations. Taking away privileges and using diversions as a tactic is an old but effective strategy. Giving and taking to create balance that gives an illusion of freedom that is elusive but obtainable is currently in use by the powers that be. Some people become successful and live extraordinary lives. Most of us, however, live our lives forever hungry for comforts that never come and hopes and dreams never realized. We refrain from rebellion for easy, uneventful, ordinary lives and submit to the powers that be as we march one by one into the grave with unfinished hopes. It is sad that we fear the unknown in life as we fear the unknown in death and choose to be meek and fear the inevitable cost. Death is owed by all and no substitutes or strong wills can in the end turn.

*

One who decides in haste brought on by passions knows all too well that living in the moment for the moment spawns a lifetime of uncontrollable consequences. One can always count on the terrible to cross the path of chance from time to time, and the terrible sometimes has permanent consequences that can affect the hasty choosers and the people around them. This alone is reason enough to stop and think about what you are doing, whom it will effect, and in the end what will be resolved or gained. It is impossible to always have a plan for every contingency, but you can have a good life philosophy that can help guide you in the difficult times and help avoid hopeless situations that are consequences to decisions made in haste brought on by passions.

*

My Great Grand Father told me
when I was a young man:
+
Love with passion.
+
Protect those you love with fierce loyalty.
+
Never make anyone your enemy on purpose.
+
Loathe your enemies avidly and with conviction,
to show them you should be respected as a
formidable adversary.
+
First impressions mean a lot but give
people you do
not know a chance.
+
Beware of pride, jealousy, wrath, lust,
and greed.
These emotions are like water:
When in control they
are serene; when out of control
they are utterly
destructive.
+
People you know to be dangerous or
foolish should
always be avoided.
+
Believe in something higher than
yourself to help

give life purpose and alleviate
some of the burden of
life's challenges and confusion.

+

Never trust entirely anything you see,
hear, or read.
Perspective gives everyone
a different point of view
and, in turn, a different story.

+

Research and learn as much as you
can on your own
and constantly challenge your
own theories and the
theories of others.

+

When proven wrong never be too
proud to admit it,
and apologize if need be. That alone
can sometimes
defuse a tense situation, and people
will respect you
greatly for that gesture.

+

Live your life by your own rules so
long as they do
not harm others.

+

Give relentless hordes that are bent
on greed and

pestilence hell, even in the face of your
own death, to
show the world your true resolve.

+

Death comes to everyone in time: Accept it,
expect it,
but do not obsess over it. People can
waste their
entire lives worrying about dangers and
variables that
may or may not lead to death or injury.
In the end, it's
better to die doing what you love than
to give up your
passions for reasons that are not your own.

*

If you choose to lead your people to a better life and tyranny is your only option to gain control or power, be prepared. When ways other than peaceful means are utilized to gain a foothold, resistance is inevitable. Even with a lifetime of struggle to compromise after the fact, many who have been wronged will never forgive. If for some reason you make it to your grave having never faced your enemies, the legacy you leave behind will not be forgotten, and somehow or someway your lifetime's gains while toiling with tyranny will be for not. In the end, the tides will change, and from your seeds of brutality will grow brutality anew. Like a pendulum the power of change causes reactions that in its end will peak and distribute power back to your enemies. In this situation you will be defeated, and your enemies will always remember you for your tyrannical tactics rather than your noble intentions.

*

Power and greed have influences that even the greatest person cannot suffer indefinitely. A simple life where people are kept busy from sunup till sundown gives mundane purpose but little fulfillment, so from tedium and dullness ambition is often born. Such people toil to ready resources and envision victory with impudent resolve. They collect power with ravenous aspiration and are afraid to lose their status, even when the end is certain. Power makes people apathetic and separates them into cliques of useful and useless. Some gather support for preposterous ideas and put them into motion to help gain power or take it away from their opposition. Others gather power by undermining the masses for self-empowerment that in the end benefit only its creator. Some implement rules and codes to create unnecessary temporary stability on areas of our lives that are best left to individual choice. Although it takes intelligence to reach one's goal in life, power and greed often influence fatuously instead of prudence. One could easily argue that this is not true, but history has proven time and time again that power corrupts, and greed is contagious.

*

Anything you work hard for but do not accomplish or possess is a test of your mettle. If you die never reaching your goal in life, your true resolve is the measure of your mettle, and no one can take that away from you, not even death. Quit without truly trying and always seek easy bounty, and your actions will brand you and indolent individual with poor resolve. Perfection is an individual perspective or perception on an object, subject, or situation. No two people will ever share the exact same opinion. If ever you hear someone speaking of achieving perfection flee.

*

Society slowly deteriorates as freedoms are sacrificed for control and false safety. Complete control always translates into oppression and in the end gives rise to a plethora of enemies who gain power with every inch of freedom taken. Complete safety can never be achieved simply because danger is always a factor in everything we do. Society needs balance, individual and common, in order to achieve longevity. When any group of people feel oppressed and has nothing to lose, they will fight to gain freedom. As a society grows, oppression turns to tyranny as freedoms are sacrificed for control in order to create stability without balance. Although this may work for many generations inevitably the oppressors' tyranny will fail to control or provide safety through stability. Without balance there can be no harmony, only chaos. In the end, society must realize that control is the easy temporary solution but not a true answer. Simply put, society needs tolerance and harmony to create stability through balance.

*

History is too often ignored in this modern world. We instinctively repeat mistakes with blind renewed hopes of a positive outcome when the past has proven, time and time again, that the path taken has failed more often than not. Politicians debate issues while problems worsen, and people die from lack of action or action applied to areas proven in the past to be useless. Our journey will end as it always has: separation of the haves and have-nots, creating rebellion or at the very least chaos. In a world of peace, physically weak but mentally superior ambitious people will grasp control and complicate the world with a constantly changing unsteady balancing act while employing a small number of the physically strong, who require direction, to enforce the wills of the establishment. The government easily forgets its primary promise as it acquires power, and it falls prey to human weaknesses that inspire poor resolve. Perhaps it is time to realize that no large group of people can be ruled fairly by an organized central force; history has proven that the greatest civilizations of the past were ruled by tyrants, but scorn has been cast on small tribes in the thicket who know little of war and technology but still manage to be content.

*

Avoiding danger at all costs is never enough; an
intelligent person who values their safety
prepares
for danger but accepts the possibility of failure.

*

Thursday

One person's pious quest for reparation is just as important as millions. Balance is easier to achieve and more humane when corrected early. When millions feel the strain of indecorous activities from apathetic wills, the changes that take place to correct these deeds are almost always catastrophic.

*

Priorities and beliefs edged in stone are an indolent person's way of dealing with life. There are a small number of cases when this philosophy on life can bring success, but it often is a lonely, obsessive existence that in the end can give rise to despair or impulsive apathetic diversions. Life is an ever changing ocean of situations that cannot be simply prioritized or dealt with using one set of beliefs. One must always have and open mind and try to understand more than one point of view. Prioritizing anything to do with people leaves someone out unintentionally and animosity can take root. Rock solid beliefs form cliques that in the end know only conflict due to close-mindedness. No single person can see much beyond their own ability to understand situations and people, but in this case prudence and tolerance should always be applied. The more we know, the more we can improvise and overcome walls of misunderstanding before it's too late.

*

People are governed by three things:
Their hearts
Their minds
Their rules
Their hearts guide with passions and
do not always
choose wisely.
Their minds calculate gains and
losses and make
decisions without compassion or empathy.
Their rules are the products of the
first two made to
govern all, regulate all, and bend all to
the hearts and
minds of the majority and those
we call leaders to help
balance society.
History, however, has proven we have
never had more
than temporary success in government
run by people.

*

Wars fought by soldiers are putrid affairs that by definition cannot be regulated. Certain groups of people, who are shortsighted, have delusions of toning down or controlling war, but these groups have always existed in history and have ignored great lessons. Soldiers are a war's raging force whose duty it is to kill and subdue the enemy at all cost. The police and guards are in place to regulate the civilian population and enforce laws after the war has been fought and won. Using soldiers as police or guards invites unfortunate avoidable circumstances. Using police or guards as soldiers will eventually invite failure due to their training, which in short, is based on control of the populace. Although every avenue should be explored to avoid war, once commitment to war has been made no expense should be spared, no rules or impediments applied to give ease to the enemy or take power away from the military to do their job in the most efficient manner possible. War is a condition that must be seen through and won by any means available. When it is over, most veterans will tell you that war is a horrible necessary evil that we as human beings tend to think of as entertaining from a distance but hell while in the mist of the fray.

*

The greatest force of change in this world comes from violent conflict. Verbal negotiations have never solved any great problems in this world, platitudes such as, "Talk is cheap" and "Actions speak louder than words" prove diplomacy is a tool for small changes. It is an unfortunate, sobering fact that we as a race cannot come to terms with out violent conflict due to difference of opinion. Most people in the world, however, know that peace is preferable, but those in power know only their own opinions and are guided by their own desires. Laws, codes, and regulations are based on the opinions of those in power over us to govern and tax as they see fit. People in power preach equality but practice segregation of the classes and keep people down to serve unknown agendas to secret ends. Conflicts are inevitable as humans are always plagued with the sickness of power, the seven sins of Western religions, apathy for others, and love only for their own desires.

*

There is a thin line between intrepidity
and fatuity
that only fate can impart.

*

Some days I find myself lost in time, confused about humanity's true purpose. The past seems like glimpses into other worlds that over time I can manipulate into different situations. I can see scenes of insignificant actions with uncertain location or time that echo in my mind for years and carry me to places of great pleasures or great pain, that forever change my desires. The world is so complex at times that I don't know what to believe and what to dismiss. Sometimes people enter my life and I know I've helped change their perceptions on certain subjects and they have in turn helped change my own. To say someone has absolute purpose is bordering on conceitedness. It seems life has no true clear meaning; we exist, and then we seem to pass on. No one can say for sure that life ends with death, but if we study nature, we see nothing is wasted. Uses for one material change its purpose in the never-ending circle of existence.

*

When it comes to the ability to achieve
or the power to
accomplish any task we have four
categories of people
to choose from:
Leaders
Followers
Survivors
Loners
Leaders seek to be elevated by
organizing followers to
complete a task at hand.
Followers seek to empower leaders
through loyalty
and trust them to lead them to victory.
Survivors think in the moment and use
anything or
anyone to gain advantages for themselves or
whomever has given them power for the
task at hand,
no matter the cost.
Loners do what they have to do to
survive without

leading or following others. A true
loner cannot be
hired but only manipulated into a task
they do not
think will benefit them.

*

More now than ever the world seems clear to me. Fear has thrown its wave over the populace and left pestilence in its wake. The meek cower in shadows and take what scraps of comfort come their way. The loner makes plans, hidden away, awaiting opportunities to flee to distant places, wild, free, and untainted by human fatuity. Others die young trying to fight against a world holding fast to the ideology of the powers that have always been. Disputes are caused by strong wills with unwavering, inflexible priorities and nonnegotiable pious beliefs. Violent conflicts spread, killing and maiming the masses, instilling desires for vengeance and wrath. Mass loathing infects the populace as people volunteer to march to their death to show their true resolve through desperate coercion. Peace has become a long forgotten word, confused with stability through tyranny. Leaders lie, soldiers die, the world suffers, and no one cares enough to stand up and say enough. Our consciences fail to quiet our pride and let loose a beast upon the world whose appetite devours everything, even until the end of all.

*

People who lack foresight for consequences of decisions made should never be given power over anyone. Having little or no ability to calculate the outcome of their choices, they leave everything to chance, leading to the opportunity for avoidable misfortune. These people should be left to their fates. To save a fool bent on control is to invite ruin.

*

When it comes right down to it, most
people project
their wills on others for no other reason
than to make
their own empty lives seem meaningful.

*

Being too honest in all situations is not always a prudent choice. It's better to be sincere in your actions, secretive in some sensitive situations, and intelligent in our choices in order to bring about a beneficial outcome for the greater good.

Of course, those who do not benefit from one set of philosophies may flourish in another.

*

Desires are too harmful to one's ability to
balance life to
be left unregulated. What one wants and
what one
needs can become blurred. Whenever you find
yourself searching for how
to choose between desire

and need, remember these words:
If it sustains you, carries you, protects you.
Keep it.
It is a need.
If it hurts you, burdens you, puts you in danger
without giving any benefit equal to
or greater than
your sacrifice.
Discard it.
It is a desire.
If you feel as if you may die without it
but deep inside
you know you will survive.
Discard it.
It is a desire.
If you derive genuine happiness from
it with little or
no personal sacrifice.
Keep it.
It is a need.
If you derive pleasure from it but never elation.
Discard it.
It is a desire.
If you believe you cannot live without it.
Keep it.
It is a need...at least for now.

*

Cruelty begets cruelty like a relentless plague. Sweeping across the soul, this plague leaves devastation in its wake. All fall to its dark influences once balance is lost and the soul is tainted. When people are completely consumed with cruelty, their pleasures are derived mostly from dark corners of the heart and mind.

*

In secret, we complain, while in public we are compliant. We shake our fist in the dark at the establishment, yet we gleefully fulfill our duties and march our children to war to show our devotion. We see the end coming and yet force no one to change our fates. In the end, we act surprised, but deep down inside we know we have condemned ourselves: a facetious farce! We prove we are sheep when we let the wolves herd us into doomed paths, picking us off one by one, no one caring until it is their turn to face the hungry beast alone. How can we be a divine species when we do nothing to avoid ruin when action is needed? In order to be more than animals we must change for the sake of our consciences and leave all stupidity to fated fools.

*

Whenever you do anything to anyone
that you would
not want done to yourself, you are a hypocrite.

*

Being lonely can come from being alone or from
being surrounded by people of
poor character who are
both unreliable and apathetic.

*

Friday

There is no limit to what you can accomplish for yourself and others in this world if you do your best to succeed. What limits you most are the things you won't try to learn when they don't come easily or take short cuts to succeed that in the end label you a charlatan.

*

Unfulfilled desires keep people mentally healthy and filled with wonder. Too much success and power give people access to their inner desires, robbing them of their dreams and innocence. When dreams become reality; we must fill the void of wonder with new fantasies. Unfortunately, when success becomes long term sometimes, the imagination cannot produce enough options to maintain balance. When harmony is lost, we draw from dark corners of the mind to compensate and create stability. What comes into the light from the darkness is not always pleasant or appropriate for others to know. Therefore, it is best to have healthy wonder rather than live out your deepest fantasies.

*

When we apply our wills to
unethical pursuits, we
lose our humanity to apathy.

*

The economy of the world is driven by greed, lust, pride, and envy. So, the query stands: How can we change and create a fair and ecological, friendly society while being driven by these ambitions? We cannot. We must change our way of thinking, our motivations, our hearts, if we are to have a positive impact on our civilization that will insure our children's freedom from this generation's convenient ignorance.

*

There are days when I doubt myself and fall prey to fear. Fear of rejection if I try and decide, out of fear, not to pursue my desires to the best of my abilities. Fear of success: What new horizons must I face once I've won the day and am looking to new challenges? Infinite scenarios fuel my fear, but more than anything I have learned this: I can either use the energy fear generates to fuel my determination or succumb and cower before obstacles and opportunities, never accomplishing greatness, dreaming of extraordinary accomplishments but never attaining them, accepting a sad life and just surviving and maintaining a common existence, hiding my talents from the world too afraid to share.

*

Guiding oneself in life is risky business but manageable with effort. Attempting to control others
is a gamble with unforeseen risks that often lead to a
myriad of consequences.

*

Accomplishments should be measured by the sense of elation and fulfillment in the individual or group who undertake the task. Whether or not it brings you glory, or riches means nothing in the presence of triumph of the spirit. We have all wasted precious time in our lives giving monumental effort to goals that do not yield desired results. A true goal gives us a feeling of self-worth and inner peace that, in the moment of realization, we could ascend to the heavens, complete. This does not mean we need to find another purpose in life once we have accomplished our goal or give up all activities once we have succeeded, but rather we must grow and aspire to become better at our calling or choose to take on other desired objectives with zeal and see them through.

*

Either you command respect for yourself or yield it to others.

*

Some are miserable in life and plant doubt in others in order to entice everyone down to join them in the depths of despair. They inject deceit into stable serene situations and ignite a fallacious fire storm of emotional destruction. When everything around them is consumed and only waste and misery remain, they feel elevated as if they have crawled out of their problematic situation on their own. These people have no internal love and cannot value others. When all is said and done, such people's souls are barren, reflecting their true intention to create misery, even unbeknownst to themselves.

*

There are those who follow the rules. To them, the law is infallible, and conscience means nothing; all they know is what the regulations dictate, what those in charge decree, and what is voted upon and passed into law.

There are those who follow their emotions and say, "Damn the rules". When a situation comes up that the rules are clear, they choose to follow another path. These people create their own way in life. Some of these people are a constant irritant to society; others are in charge of it and spend their lives creating the rules for others to follow.

*

Atonement cannot be based on outside judgment. People must create stability within themselves and forgive internally. Everyone makes mistakes in life, and no one is immune. In some cases, self-forgiveness is improbable, let alone forgiveness for those who have been wronged. If you truly feel forgiveness cannot be obtained, then you must learn to accept the consequences of your actions in a way that you feel is appropriate. Take from your and others' experiences in life and grow spiritually and mentally so, you can evolve into a greater person than you were yesterday.

*

The difference between someone who values
you and someone who loves you are simple.
You are valued for what you can do,
what you can
produce, and your dependability to
create a constant
positive result.
You are loved by those who care not what you
can do,
produce, or create but only care that
you are there,
happy, and comfortable.

*

We replace wonder with fact and ideas with disciplined faith, and cannot comprehend where all this animosity originates. 'Wonder' has no facts to discourage or disappoint others because it bases itself on ideas. Ideas can change and be molded into whatever is necessary, while disciplined faith has no room for change accept by its great leaders who are normally chosen for their steadfast ideology. When we cannot or are told by influential individuals not to accept another group or individual, we find ourselves part of a disciplined faith that excludes outsiders and their ideas as wrong and dismisses their wonder as fatuity. We insult them unintentionally, causing anger to be directed at our complacency. Ideas and wonder should be shared in peaceful communion, and all should walk away with respect for their own ideas and new found respect for others without the need to convert or prove people wrong.

*

Betrayal is worth a plethora of pain to the loyal.

*

Once scorned, a person may take revenge or offer forgiveness when given the opportunity. All forgiveness by human beings are subject to be retracted when not infused with sincerity. If you seek forgiveness, be prepared to make amends. If you want to face wrath, it takes little effort to push a wronged soul over the edge into the realm of vengeance.

*

Instead of trying to understand others,
blind pious
purpose motivates manipulative individuals
who seek
to regulate all in the righteous quest to
convert the

world and save and masses from their free-thinking foolishness.

*

Pride can cause us to make regrettable decisions. We can abandon important responsibilities and invent justifications to support our prideful choices. With pride, we guide ourselves into an abyss of regret if ever we grow to comprehend our folly fully. The great emotion of pride must be resisted for the greater good of the person and the people around them it affects. All people in all positions should be leery of pride's trap and know that it has been labeled dangerous by religion, philosophy, and psychology for a good reason.

*

After living on this earth for a number of years, I have come to the conclusion that I am alone. No one can see through my eyes, no one feels my pain, no one cares when I cry aloud; people only wish I would stop and deal with my pain in a manner they believe is appropriate. Loneliness is central in our lives, yet we exhaust endless energy to distract ourselves from this fact and are surrounded by others also seeking momentary relief. We are born into a world where we never truly see ourselves, only images and reflections. What I see through my eyes no one else can imagine, how I interpret information in my mind no one else can conceive. Though I write these words that you can read, do you identify with my point of view? Do not feel uneasy about being misunderstood or alone, but know that this is the natural state of the world. Some of us have the skills to delude ourselves into thinking little of the loneliness and become lost in worldly diversions; others know the pain of loneliness and are often consumed by it.

*

Surviving a life of turmoil or living in blissful balance can lead to longevity, but too many harsh extremes and misfortune leads to destruction, which in the end can lead to an early demise.

*

Saturday

The past cannot be changed. Accept it,
learn from it, and
do your best to come to terms with it.
The future
cannot be foretold. Accept it and
apply your lessons
from the past to help produce a positive
outcome no
matter the circumstances you may
find yourself in.

*

Brooding over anything that has already grown into a situation that cannot be changed or that requires more resources than you have to resolve should be left to take its course despite the outcome. We all must prepare for the inevitable and accept our fate no matter how unpleasant it maybe. We can choose to fight against impossible odds to meet our fate on our own terms or lay down and concede to our end in whatever fashion fate has chosen. Struggling for stolen moments of temporary relief shows desperation toward what we wish to flee but are destined to face.

*

When someone loves themselves, you can tell by their capacity to understand others and make people around them feel loved. When someone does not love themselves, you can tell by their obsessive control over others instead of love for who they are. Simply put, when someone loves themselves, love comes from within. When someone does not love themselves, love comes from outside sources and pleasures.

*

Good habits require discipline, but bad habits are simply human defaults requiring little or no effort to maintain, inspired by indolent methods that, most of the time, can be easily defined as successful blind endeavors or facetious attempts ending in catastrophe.

*

In a perfect world a gifted person is prosperous without standing on other people's shoulders, but rather by standing tall and in those moments be noticed, and recognized. Such people influence others to take successful courses of action then settle back down on their own feet to join the triumphant journey. The gifted should never take preference above others who have taken their advice and prospered less or the ones who have not taken the advice and suffered or even still the others who have succeeded differently than proposed from the beginning.

*

Have...
Confidence in who you are.
Commitment to your objectives.
Perseverance to overcome your trials and tribulations along the way.
Knowledge to adapt if your ideas
are no longer
practical in this world or you
simply change your
mind.

*

Life is all about experiences; we grow and
triumph by them
or we fail and fall into chaos by them.

*

Humans are at their best when confronted by a common opposition requiring unity. When times are stable, people compete for status and oppress and hurt one another for the need of purpose. The elusive meaning of life is ever clear during times of peril and infinitely obscure during times of tranquility.

*

Saying anything destructive may help
alleviate your

own stress, but it creates animosity in the situation and makes amends improbable.

*

Once you become aware of your own existence, life becomes priceless. As time grinds on, our mortality becomes painfully clear, and we all fear the inevitable but know we must succumb. Some desperately cling to life due to fear of the unknown; others greet death with a sigh of relief that their pain has finally come to an end.

*

You are defined by your actions. Your words, however, announce or mask your true intentions.

*

The wicked rule with fear and apathy.
The weak submit to cowardice.
'The self-righteous struggle to control everything with little or no success.
The good battle all, but to no avail.

*

Desperation, necessity, and desire are unsafe motivations.

*

Most people spend their lives engrossed in distracting

pleasures that gain them little more than
fleeting moments
of satisfaction.

*

Before you go off and maliciously slander
others, be
prepared to also be the victim of spiteful
prattle.

*

You should never give expression to any of your powerful emotions in the moment that you feel them. In most situations, it is best to evaluate your problem as a whole, logically explore your feelings, and make a conclusion based on facts, all the while staying silent, even if you feel distress. Speaking your heart too often will alert others to your emotional state and they will know you are defined by your heart and cannot always be trusted in sensitive situations. Exhibit too much control and people will fear your mastery over your emotions, labeling you emotionally barren. Balance is simply being human, making mistakes, never being too proud to apologize when needed and being silent when silence is called for.

*

When you are young it is time to explore your soul, experiment with your desires, and reach your goals so you can fulfill your dreams and live life to the fullest.

When you have succeeded and feel content with your accomplishments, it is time to bond with others; create deep personal attachments to responsible, loyal individuals; give love and support to them; and receive it in return. Without first learning to love yourself and complete your soul, you can never be fully devoted to anyone.

*

If you are truly secure in your beliefs,
you will not need
an army of followers to change the world or
loyal praises for confirmation.
Security in your own beliefs gives you
harmony and in
turn fullness in life, no one can
cast doubt upon.

*

Those who can articulate themselves well are
worth
their weight in gold among talkers.
Those who take quick, unguided action are
priceless
among the impatient.
Those who speak when something
needs to be said
and takes action when action is needed
are often the
vessels of our ideals.

*

Hope is often born of desperation,
but without hope
desperation turns to hopelessness, from there,
despair, and ultimately failure.
To try despite overwhelming odds has always
been the greatest test to historical figures who
sought to heal the world or sought its ruin.
Hope has served both hero and villain in the
ongoing struggle of life. So, that one person's
hopes can be another person's nightmare can
accurately be called a fact.
The strength and determination
of one person's
hopes can influence virtuous results or great
atrocities.
Choose!

*

Worthy people are cast aside whilst compliant
followers eager to serve lead us all to ruin.

*

When you betray others for gain, you are indeed
untrustworthy, greedy, and weak. When you
betray
yourself and your personal beliefs for
gain you are a
tool for the betrayer, and you are
less valued than
the resources your masters gave you to control.

*

Simple people seek power over others for selfish reasons, forged by desires and planted by apathy.

*

Small minds apply small ideas to complicated problems with so much zeal that problems change but are never solved. Small minds, however, announce the change as a step in the right direction toward the true solution, never admitting their folly for fear of discovery of failure brought about by pride.

*

With pitchers of poisonous potions, you may
wrestle
your way to power, but your soul will find its
way
to ruin.

*

Human beings bury themselves in ignorance,
leading
themselves to ruin for comforts
in exchange for
compliance to avaricious apathetic
guidance that
serves the tyranny of the pride of fools.

*

No time too soon will come to end the
tyranny of
greed.

*

If given a choice between justice and
vengeance for
transgressions of an immoral nature, I choose
vengeance. Justice is balanced revenge and
normally
does not bring the personal satisfaction that
vengeance has to offer.
Unfortunately, vengeance disrupts the balance in
one's soul and does not endure the
long term. Justice
forces forgiveness or brings balance, and
vengeance
creates satisfaction at a price too high
for most to
balance, and it holds tight to unforgiving
ideology.
I choose vengeance because part of me is lost.

*

Fools often live delusional lives.

*

Ideas that are based on ignorance are always
oppressive.

*

Sunday

Because we leave complicated matters to small people, we suffer the fate of fools.

*

The very moment you start assessing any group of people based on a few experiences in your own life and the experiences of others who are like-minded, welcome to the world of prejudice. A closed mind is not just the result of one opinion but is also a result of collective reasoning based on self-righteousness and enforced by desires of control rather than understanding.

*

It is better to over think a problem than
to suffer the
consequences of not planning enough.

*

There is no person in my life that I feel a great amount of admiration, envy, or pride. I feel good for anyone who succeeds and finds joy, I feel empathy and concern for those who fail in life or who suffer for reasons not of their making. Those who take a course that hurt others for gain, however, deserve little more than my contempt, even if they find themselves suffering.

*

Know yourself
Know your dreams
Understand the consequences of good intentions.
Choose!

*

When human existence ends, it will be hard to cry for us; the earth will let out a sigh of relief as balance is restored to nature.

*

The inequality of civilization is the key cause of our greatest discord. A foundation of sharing resources and providing the basics can help create a peaceful society if humans could control their greed and pride. When we stand at the starting line of life in a staggered arrangement but move in a straight line toward the finish line, it is easy for those who are back the furthest to give up. To expect everyone to achieve the same measure in life when starting from different points is ignorance. Few people are driven; we look for our dreams and are discouraged when we see how long the journey is. On our life journey, we begin to battle trials and tribulations and when we find comfort along the way, never completing our trek, but instead finding stability. When successful people ramble on with platitudes and unreal ideologies and delusions about possible achievements in situations with few attainable goals, it leads, upon failure, to suffering that can easily be defined as misery; in truth, this is most of us. With a world based on greed, inequality, prejudice, violence, it is easy to hide away with adequate resources to weather the storm and hope when it is over a better time emerges from the ruin, but has this ever been so? It is unlikely that the world will change its ways because human beings often think too much of themselves, especially while in a group, judging and condemning others with ignorance. It is always dangerous to look at any situation from just one angle and sometimes best to be tolerant. You may never understand some situations no matter how empathetic you think you are. In so many words, as long as we are separated into classes and profit from misery and hope, we are guilty. This leads us to not have a civilization but rather a competition which only leads to inequality and, in turn, discord.

*

Human predators and monsters have always existed in disguises so deceiving that no one is immune in identifying the danger accurately. The problem lies not in the identification of the individuals but rather the recognition of such characters inside one's self. Weakness and cruelty are animal traits that humans take to new levels. We create elites and fill them with pride and call for protection from tyrants we once held in high regard. When we look in the mirror and see ourselves as righteous and judge others for situations, we ourselves do not understand, we are guilty of ignorance personified. When this happens, we have come full circle and find ourselves serving dark leaders to secret agendas masked by good intentions with obvious prejudices. Hypocrisy rear its ugly head as blind loyalty leads people down easy paths with the promise of better tomorrow's, which reflect all our deceiving yesterdays but are remembered as triumphs of the good.

*

Time is our most valuable asset. Talents are worth nothing if they are not useful or profitable. Your life has value only when coupled with a use. Some people have no time to spare for civilizations' desires and others refuse to give time for money and amenities. For this, they are looked down upon by society: they do not contribute to the great failed experiment. Choose to value yourself above contributing to civilization and you will be the subject of cruelty fueled by control masked by righteousness. We are little more than slaves to a system that steals our time in exchange for nothing more valuable than someone else agenda fulfilled. In essence, you are only as valuable as your ability to produce a positive outcome for powers you do not understand but support in exchange for small wealth. This loosely equates to sacrificing part of your life for others' programs of greed.

*

In today's society there is no future for expression or freedom. In the guise of freedom and independence, the world sells us debt, fear, and dependence-with no guarantee of satisfaction. Our future is sacrificed to the powers that be; they consume and control as they see fit. The elite fight with great zeal to push their agendas, all the while repressing any idea that creates more freedom or happiness they do not approve of. They separate, aggravate to create tension, and lie to our faces about their true intentions. They besmirch those whose ideas seem threatening to their opinions, and they rally others who believe the same but are actively opposed to their perceived enemies' ideas. We let ourselves be coerced into inflexible positions based on untrustworthy individuals' theories with an apathetic intentions that we falsely believe are benign in nature. As long as we praise fools whose agenda is slavery through debt, fear, and dependence, we will always be gleeful servants to the tyranny of prejudice concepts of cowardly cretins.

*

Whilst among imbeciles, who believes in the prospect of eternity considering the brevity mortality gives to life, which is filled with the terrible more often than with fortune. Wish instead for benevolence so that eternity is not paved with reasons to hope but rather reasons to rejoice.

*

Review Requested:

We'd like to know if you enjoyed the book.
Please consider leaving a review on the platform
from which you purchased the book.

CPSIA information can be obtained
at www.ICGtesting.com
Printed in the USA
LVHW101250300323
742972LV00005B/550

9 781682 355701